"Poems by
Tom Holt"

"Poems by Tom Holt"

by

TOM HOLT

Introduction by
Edward Lucie-Smith

M & J Hobbs
in association with
Michael Joseph

First published in Great Britain by M & J Hobbs
25 Bridge Street, Walton-on-Thames
in association with Michael Joseph Ltd
52 Bedford Square, London, W.C.1
1973

ISBN 0 7181 1181 8

Set and printed in Great Britain by Ebenezer Baylis & Son Ltd.,
The Trinity Press, Worcester, and London
in Ehrhardt twelve on thirteen point on paper
supplied by Book Papers Ltd and bound by
Dorstel Press, Harlow

Contents

Introduction

Children's poetry is a thornier subject than it appears to be at first sight. Are we, for example, to attempt to read it as we would any other poetry, or are we to value it chiefly for the insights that it offers into childhood? During the present century, and especially during the last two decades, the tendency has been to lay special emphasis on the value of childishness; just as there has been a parallel tendency to exalt the value of madness. Children and madmen, so we are told, have an easier access to certain kinds of truth. This view goes a little beyond the one which is traditionally embodied in the story of the emperor's new clothes, where the child alone is sufficiently unsophisticated to expose a fraud which everyone else accepts. The claim is that children, in their use of words (as, too, in their use of pictorial images) can strike through to emotions and ideas which shock us with their purity and freshness, and make us, thanks to this shock, reconsider our own assumptions. A number of fascinating collections of children's poetry have been published in recent years, the most famous and the most controversial being, perhaps, Christopher Searle's anthology *Stepney Words*.

This is not a book of that kind, for two reasons. The first and most obvious is that the poems in it are not the work of children, but of one child—Tom Holt, who wrote them between the ages of nine and eleven. The second is that it is the work of a professional writer, and not of amateurs. But just a moment— can one really claim "professionalism" for a child of Tom Holt's present age in any activity, much less in poetry? Until I read this manuscript, I should have been doubtful. I recognise, of course, that there are gifted child actors; and, even more so, child musicians. But the framework for their activity is external, and provided by adults. The musical child prodigy, such as the young Mozart, is a phenomenon that we accept, because it recurs with reasonable regularity. If we now see such prodigies less often upon the concert platform, it is because the parents of such children now prefer, and one would think wisely, that they should cultivate their gift under less strenuous conditions.

Tom Holt's poetry, however, strikes me as genuinely professional because he seems to work on the principles we discover in the work of adults. These are not naive poems, occasionally illuminated by some marvellous line or phrase. Tom Holt has a perfect command of the basic mechanisms of the language, more so, indeed, than many adults who call themselves writers. While it is true that modern poetic technique is in some respects less demanding than technique of a more traditional kind, with its emphasis on rhyme and on regular metre, these poems are nevertheless very much within the writer's control. He is able to aim for a particular effect, and to produce it. More important than this, these are poems in which we find a striking stylistic continuity. Having read one, we tend to recognise different aspects of the same poetic personality in all the others.

In order to try and define the kind of poetry this is, one or two comparisons are in order. Here, for example, is a poem by that extraordinarily appealing child Marjory Fleming, who died in 1811, when she was just a month short of her ninth birthday:

> Three turkeys fair their last have breathed
> And now this world forever leaved
> Their Father & their Mother too
> Will sigh and weep as well as you
> Mourning for their osprings fair
> Whom they did nurse with tender care
> Indeed the rats their bones have cranched
> To eternity are they launched
> There graceful form and pretty eyes

Their fellow fows did not despise
A direful death indeed they had
That would put any parent mad
But she was more than usual calm
She did not give a single dam
She is as gentel as a lamb
Here ends this melancholy lay
Farewell Poor Turkeys I must say

Read one of Tom Holt's poems, and you enter into an entirely different and far more sophisticated world of thinking and feeling:

Before, now, after,
Now and then,
In the night of the sea
And the power of the land
Is no failing . . .

I have deliberately chosen a fairly early example. The difference in age between the two poets is, in this instance, only about two years.

A more testing comparison is provided by the earliest poems of William Blake, first published in 1783, but apparently composed from 1769 onwards—that is, from the author's twelfth year. Unfortunately it is a little difficult to be certain which poems in the collection *Poetical Sketches* are the earliest, but here is a specimen, by no means the best, but also by no means the least successful:

To Morning
O holy virgin! clad in purest white,
Unlock heav'n's golden gates and issue forth;
Awake the dawn that sleeps in heaven; let light
Rise from the chambers of the east, and bring
The honied dew that cometh on waking day.
O radiant morning, salute the sun,
Rouz'd like a huntsman to the chace, and, with
Thy buskin'd feet, appear upon our hills.

9

Look from this to the poetry contemporary with it, that is, to the poetry of 1769 or the early 1770s; and look from Tom Holt's poems to the poetry of the 1970s, and which seems more remarkable? The answer cannot really be in doubt.

I realise that by suggesting that the reader compare Tom Holt's work with so great a genius as Blake, I have entered upon dangerous ground. No admirer of these poems—and clearly I am an admirer—would want to see the writer with the label "genius" tied round his neck. It is much too early to tell whether or not Tom Holt has genius. Indeed, it is too early to say if he will go on writing poetry, or turn to something quite different. Few little boys who want to be engine-drivers finish up driving engines. The point is that these are, on the whole, good poems taken just as they are; and that the circumstances in which they have been produced are both fascinating and extraordinary.

Not the least extraordinary thing about them is that they precede the psychic and physical upheaval of adolescence. Most teachers will tell you that very young children write poems—poems of a kind—without inhibition or difficulty. Then comes a period when the practice of poetry makes them feel self-conscious. Often this period begins around the age of ten or eleven, and continues into the early teens. Those who will be adult poets often begin to write again when they are about fourteen. I know that this was the time when I myself first began to write poetry in any serious spirit, and I seem to remember that most of my contemporaries have told me much the same story.

Almost the classic example of the connection between poetry and puberty is Arthur Rimbaud. The poetic personality explodes into being as the physical change takes place. In the circumstances, one would imagine that Rimbaud's poetry, produced from the age of fourteen onwards, and Tom Holt's would be very different. Yet, when I first read Tom's manuscript, I was struck by a passage that seemed familiar:

As the battle rages, by the wood
Where the bullets fly, there is a flower
In full blossom, white in colour,
Its delicate leaves face the sky,
And beside it lies the corpse of a soldier,
Whose head is beaten in with the butt of a gun,
A bayonet wound staining his grey uniform.

At first I thought of Robert Frost:

The battle rent a cobweb diamond-strung
And cut a flower beside a ground bird's nest
Before it stained a single human breast.

Later, it seemed obvious that the resemblance was to Rimbaud's *Le Dormeur du Val:*

C'est un trou de verdure où chante une rivière
Accrochant follement aux herbes des haillons
D'argent; où le soleil, de la montagne fière,
Luit: c'est un petit val qui mousses de rayons.
Un soldat jeune, bouche ouverte, tête nue,
Et la nuque baignant dans le frais cresson bleu,
Dort; il est étendu dans l'herbe, sous la nue,
Pâle dans son lit vert où la lumière pleut.

(It is a green hollow where a river sings
Madly catching on the grasses
Silver rags; where the sun shines from the proud
    mountain:
It is a small valley which bubbles over with rays.

A young soldier, his mouth open, his head bare,
And the nape of his neck bathing in the cool blue
    watercress,

Sleeps; he is stretched out on the grass, under
    clouds,
Pale on his green bed where the light rains down.)
                                    (trans. Wallace Fowlie)

Later still, I discovered that Tom hasn't yet read
Rimbaud.

Yet the resemblance is, I think, more than coinci-
dental. What both these young poets have is a sense
of tragedy, of human littleness:

> My life is a curtained window,
> A refraction of light in the mirror.
> I am a flash in a snow-covered field,
> Brilliant in brightness,
> Not a torch in the mist
> But in clear daylight.

The conventional "innocence" and "happiness" of
childhood are just as far away from Tom Holt's
poems as they are from Rimbaud's, without Rim-
baud's desperate experiences to account for the loss.

Of course, the differences are just as important as
the similarities. Rimbaud's ambition not merely to
rival God, but to become God, is not present. How
alarming it would be if it were! There is nothing
which in the least resembles the mingled bitterness
and nostalgia of Rimbaud's *Les Poêtes de sept ans*. In
fact, childhood itself, as a subject, is strikingly absent.
You cannot look back on something, consider it,
sum it up, judge it, regret it, when you are still in the
very midst of it. Recently I asked Tom why he didn't
try his hand at a brief autobiography. Oh, he protested,
there was nothing to say. That would not be the adult
view.

Nevertheless, besides being interesting poems in
their own right, which is the primary reason for
reading them, these are reports from a world from
which we seldom receive such complex and such solid
information—the world of pre-adolescence. The

information is filtered in various ways—through the individuality of a remarkable rather than an average child, far ahead of his contemporaries in intellectual development. And also through the poets Tom has read. We catch echoes of Eliot, for example, and of Ted Hughes. But there is a core which no literary influence seems to have reached or affected. It is not the least remarkable thing about a remarkable book.

Edward Lucie-Smith

"Poems by
Tom Holt"

The Poem and the Bird

I know a poem
About the burying of a young
Dead sparrow.
It is a fine, intricate poem
And it has never
Been written down.
It is titled:
My heart,
God have mercy
Upon us all,
Every one.

1971

Pity a Worm

Condemn him to the lower depths,
Drop him in the pit of hell,
Stamp on his hands as he tries to climb;
But yet the damned will stand.

He has no hope in life,
A thing beyond all hate,
As he crawls back
To be disturbed once more
Condemn him not.

He does not look for help,
Expects no kindnesses,
He has a kind of world
So leave him that
And pity him.

1972

Headache

I am trapped by my head only
In this crushing pile-driver of tension.
My brain is rotting in my head,
I cannot think,
I cannot move,
I am a worm with half its body crushed,
Pulses of power rock my agonised nerve-centres,
My temples swim with loose liquid,
I am a house divided:
My head will split, like a plain
Broken by an earthquake.

If the insensate head were to fall
Like a tree's dead leaves,
Breaking off cleanly,
There would be relief, or so it seems.

1972

Desirable Property

He sold us a charming plot of ground
On which stood this Very Desirable Residence;
But he did not tell us how he drove out
The ancient dwarves,
He didn't say that he had drained the lake
Where lived the pure white swans,
Nor did he tell us how
He chopped down the magic grove.
Had we known how he had defaced the hills,
Denuded the valley and destroyed the trees
Then how could we have borne to live
In that sweet house
With roses round the door.

1972

Light

I

I cannot see the images
Now the fire is dead,
They were vivid.
Fire's eternal ascension
Controlled by the barriers
Of time, position
And mood,
The death of fire
Reluctant to pass,
These were the facts
Of candle-light.

II

When death is blurring
The life-long candles,
Fire rises to its own position
To be snatched down by reality
In its prime
And expires, the phoenix
Of our existence,
And from the ashes
Rises a new form
To shorten the life
Of the species.
But in death
The candle is extinguished
So I cannot see the reason.

1972

Shadow

Shadow is not a pretence of the man
Only a disciple: sadly he is sometimes
Better than that he follows, he carries
A handsome form but has no heart to be of iron,
No mind to lodge envy and hate
However bright the sun.

1973

Realisation

Slumped on his goatskin bed
The Zarchar is resting,
Here after the battle
Is the great general Olac.
But beyond the victory and the wooden gods
Are further thoughts:
He has seen life and death
In a burning circle
But did not realise
That death and life exist.
Life was everlasting,
Still young,
Unlike the dribbling, shrivelled elders
Sitting round the fire remembering.
His eyes are full, theirs are empty,
Their pupils eaten away with seeing.
Their minds are full, there is no space
Left in them for the future.
He envies the sleeping hound at his feet,
The rough black pony stamping outside,
Because they do not know
They are alive.
For the bronze goddess is misted
With its polish not wiped clean,
The sacred ram has a broken stand
Tied together with cord.
Olac has discovered Mortality.

1973

Again

I do not know why I turned;
From a sixth sense, bidding me look again,
Or from a hope my search was ended.
But was there something I should have seen,
Some small happening I would later discover?
Was it the foundation of a new civilisation
Or the destruction of our present life?
Perhaps some deity pulled me round,
Said 'Gaze upon your future,
It is there.'
I do not know of what value
My second glance was
But let me rest assured, I am not changed.

1972

Conquerors

In this age of realism
One's heart is stirred by talk
Of Poetry. Nothing is left
Of the old formal Empire,
Writing by the rule book,
Yet the resistance is working
Against the army of the realists.
They are fighting to restore
Some poetry to the world.

1971

Suicide

There was an ancient salesman
Who waited by the quay,
'By thy long black hair and leathern case
Now wherefore stoppest thou me?'

What is the map's tale?
It knows the secrets of the world,
In four corners it holds
The passion of the world.
Can the map tell
The need of man to join God
In God's house;
Girl in a church
Lays flowers on the altar
'On Jesus' dressing table,
So that he can see them
When he wakes up'.
When will he wake up?

If I were a rich man
I would hire assassins to kill me;
Then I would hire a bodyguard
And sit back
And watch them fight it out.

The elastic clock stretches forward,
When you go slowly
The elastic stretches,
Waste your time and it will slow down,
When it bends
Don't relax the catch
Or your life will fly away.
It will go and you can't get another,
They are rare, going off the market,
Save yours, it will do you good,
Life is good for you.

Here we go round the atom bomb, the atom bomb,
the atom bomb,
How can we stop the holocaust at five o'clock in the
morning?

1971

Ghosts

Ghosts inhabit crowds;
Look around and you will see them,
Many thousands,
Each with a hell of his own.
Ghosts inhabit trains,
Disguised as your reflection
   in the window;
You see yourself
And the ghost is doomed
To be you, to move
In your style.
Ghosts make up the world,
The world is full of ghosts
That never lived before.

1971

Furies

Truth behind the wall,
Truth around the corner
Dropping its shadow
In the dark midnight;
Conscience takes the form
Of cupboards and of windows,
Of the one bright star outside,
Of strange but explainable noises.
They come only to him
Who wants them,
Not consciously on the surface
But in the inwardness of guilt.
He expects them
As an old man expects death,
He knows them
As he knows a friend,
He does not worry about
Their coming but is only curious.
He has compassion now,
Now that he must.
Even if he does not know the Truth,
Even if he was not at fault,
He still would pay
For fear of Them
And give the gods their sport,
Like the hunter who does not hunt
Lest he spoils the king's pleasure.

1972

Relaxation

Watch the sun setting
Above the hill of our contrivances;
Has it been so bad a day
As we come to consider it?
Now that the leopard's changed his spots,
Now that the sun is gone,
As you lie in your bed
And think
Was it as bad as all that?
Really?

1971

Death-Cycle

Moss on the rusty helmet,
Insects in the comfort of the boots,
Fragments of clothing in the nests of birds,
Flies finding easy food,
A spider's web between the feet
And a lizard at home in the skull.
This man was not wasted,
He provided comfort, home and food
For the creatures of the field,
A compensation
For destruction,
From one death
Is formed many lives.
Life is the same
In man or fly or bird,
Nature restores herself
And life and death are one in the field.

1972

The Facts of Life

I am not a student of science
But I know a little physics:
The reaction between two emotions,
Which shall remain nameless,
Meet in silence
When time is still.
Neither do I know much about law,
But I know that one law must be kept:
When two certain emotions meet
It is illegal to interfere with their progress.
I am no great lover of statues,
But there are monuments raised
To those specific emotions
And these must never be defaced.
I know these two emotions do not haunt
Most men, but they haunt me,
And, with that little science, that little law
    and that small remnant of culture
I keep myself from death.

1972

The Judgement of a Soul

I

The day is passing
Into the oblivion of late post-meridian
By the old trees that died
Oh, so long ago
And passed to the land of the mindless
For no one gave trees free-will.
There sleeps a being
At his last hour after relief
From his fleshly coffin,
Resting in Death's hotel,
Well, it is expected,
He must reserve his strength
For the trial of a soul.

After the occasion, the count.

II

Hell is not a red room
Brimming with fire,
Silence, impossible for screams and groaning.
Hell is the complaining,
    the impatience,
    the indignation and the non-comprehension,
All suspense, hate, ungratefulness.
Hell is people like you
    being like you,
Hell is meeting yourself
    mirrored in others,
Hell is mirroring others.
The realisation
And expression of your own desires.

III

Wait! I am being hasty,
I have heard rumours,
Rumours of a story,
A new handful of straws to clutch at.
I have heard that the Christ
Rose from Hell after three days,
He was here, surely
He will have mercy
Knowing what it is like.
Yet . . .
    He knows all,
Why should one thing concern Him
    More than another,
Why should He care about anything?
On whose information was this thing based?
Still,
    A straw is better than nothing
If no return to faith . . .
                    You did not
Start the rumour.

No feast without cost.

IV

Heaven's gates are opened on the sight,
Here is Limbo,
Here we queue for judgement.
Now we hope,
            Now we pray,
Now we remember how we doubted the rumour.
Now we discuss each other's chances,
Here we are hopeful for each other
Because we do not want
To wreck our own chances
By being proud,
Though we care not if another fails

Because of pride . . .
My turn soon.
The sky is blue here
Not black,
It is cool here
Not humid.
The person in front goes in . . .
Think of something else,
Now, now, now, now it is me . . .

After the feast, the payment.

1972

Time and Space

Before, now, after,
Now and then,
In the night of the sea
And the power of thc land
Is no failing.

The cross in Christ
And the cross in man,
All together in a cross
Is no failing.

All to fire
All to God
Is no failing.

All falls
For the last spate of justice
To mourn now, to hate before, to think not of after.

As it was in the beginning,
Is not now,
And never shall be
In the end.

1971

Death is a state

Death is a state that is arbitrary
And it is proven that all are dead
To the chosen *lifeless*, the immortal,
Those unlucky are dead
To the stupid life-holders
The dead are finished,
Dead.
Thus dead kill dead.

I watch, I wait,
I never win,
I hunt and never
Kill. Running
They dodge my spear,
My arrows miss
For they are protected.

Life is but a useless struggle,
We fight, we die,
We die.
Why die rich?
Why die old?
Death is arbitrary
Also.

1971

Thought (I)

Thought is a long-boat paddling through the shallows,
Slow boat moving on the docile stream.
Time cannot rule thought,
Can thought rule time?

No matter how it comes, the thought comes,
In a flash, or with the slow boat,
Coming with the tide and the dusk.
Wait for dusk for thought,
Wait for eternity for inspiration.

1971

Then Absolution

I was never content
With the absolute maximum,
It was always too much,
Yet too little,
Never perfect
In either direction.
Always the necessity
To express one's views
To a brick wall
That does not respond
When you are wrong.
I would rather see
The Inferno swelling red
Inside the chamber of my perfection,
Bringing everything to dust,
For only in dust can one see
One's achievements.
For everything is dust,
Refined, compressed,
Only the elements
Are not composed of dust,
There is not much left
After that great reduction.
And the world can be reduced
To nothing by the mind
Of the philosopher,
The world, the smallest bone
In the skeleton
Of Eternity.

1972

Pretence is what you call

I

Pretence is what you call
A novel weapon
In the way of weapons,
As patience and perfection,
The last piece of iron
To be smelted
The last piece of wood
To be burnt,
The last candle to be extinguished.
This is the battle
That is fought by Pretence,
Pretence of patience.

II

Humanity is a desert
That lasts as far
    as the eye
      can
      see.
Civilisation is a loneliness
With no one there
    to be seen.
Death is an isolation
When the echo
    resounds
      against the wall.

III

The graven image
    is ironed out
    to be the
    onlyonethatisalltogether
And when the death is done
    Life is again.

1972

Dulce Domum

The old man sits in the shade
Remembering when fields ranged out
From the quiet village,
Where farmers grazed the cattle
Silently rejoicing in the spring air,
The newly reborn hedges
Crying out in the mimicked voice of birds,
Birds that audaciously preached
Cheerful resistance to knowledge and change.
But then a war came
                    So he marched away.
How it all looked the same
Still, the cattle, hedges and birds.
Like a church fête or a fair, recruiting started,
(How far from war was this illusion)
Men marching away as if to harvest.
Boats, barges and the sea,
Like a blue cover on a man's bed,
Writhing as Poseidon twitched and moved,
Then the war, the guns, the shadows,
And he pondered:
                    These men he fought and never saw
Had marched from their village across the sea.
At home the fields were overgrown,
Corn rotted and gates mouldered,
The spring was here, birds sang
And the weed-choked hedges still smiled,
Eyes like wild poppies and a mouth of white daisies,
Many were dead
                    But many lived on,
Changes, but not felt, continued.
Twenty or thirty years went past before
He noticed he was again at war.
Now he was too old
                    To see his friends die in France,
So he joined the Home Guard with the others.
It was spring again, but new birds sang,

Bombers and fighters, winding like flies with thick black
     tails.
How comical they looked,
Half dressed in khaki, half in oldest clothes,
Pitchforks and axes, hoes and shotguns now
To drive the enemy away, perhaps by hoping,
These old men in their innocence
Thinking they could save their country—
Still, beer was rationed, the village green was ploughed.
The war passed.
                    Now times changed.
Instead of mushrooms factories grow in Willow Field,
And Farmer Myles bought machinery and went to
     conferences.
He had never been from home, save when he went to
     France,
But now he lived in an old folks' council flat.
Yes, it was better
              To live on his black and white memories of
     childhood,
His naive illusions of how it was better,
Than to risk living it again
                    And ruin them.

1973

Beyond

Beyond the dungeon wall are the wide fields,
Green and airy where the sheep graze
And birds sing in a cheerful tone;
Each little blade of grass
Is alive, each tiny fly
Lives its own life, oblivious of man.
Amid the waving trees
Squirrels leap in a perpetual game,
Audacious sparrows fly, singing.

Beyond the hills, the bay,
And after, the green and friendly sea,
Leading on, mile after mile,
To the wide plains of the ocean.
There is the realm of albatross and whale,
Echoing to the gull's cry and the splash
Of the playful dolphin.
On the horizon, where sea and sky
Are joined, are foreign isles
Of dark-skinned merchants and green jungles,
Of gaudy coloured birds and dazzling flowers,
Vast lands of palms and foliage
Fading against the mountains,
Whose heads are as white
As those of the Elders,
And above, Elysium,
Paradise, which holds a mirror
To the free fields, the rolling oceans,
The vast forests and the dazzling beauties.

The dungeon has a gate called Death,
Beyond it, the fields and oceans,
Much greener and brighter
Now they are in your grasp.

1972

Black

Black houses
    littering
Black streets,
    Put there by town councils in a
Black mood;
Black looks,
Black Magic
    chocolate boxes strewn around;
Black doctors
    with
Black bags;
Black Marias
    chasing
Black-hearted robbers
    going into
Black oblivion
    until the fuss dies down.
Black look-out
    for
Black London.

1971

Musketry

As the battle rages, by the wood
Where the bullets fly, there is a flower
In full blossom, white in colour,
Its delicate leaves face the sky,
And beside it lies the corpse of a soldier,
Whose head is beaten in with the butt of a gun,
A bayonet wound staining his grey uniform.
This is a young man, who yesterday
Sang on the road as he marched,
Had no hate for the men he killed,
Or for those who killed him.
He joined the army to escape the law,
A death either way, dead by
The heap of corpses in the wood
At Lookout Hill.

1970

The Apple Tree

There is an apple tree
Outside in the garden,
Its leaves cover the ground in autumn;
When it drops its leaves the tree weeps,
Calling them back, to make them fall again.

Men are like the apple tree
Outside in the garden:
Corpses cover the ground in war-time;
When it loses its young men the world weeps,
Calling them back to give them glory.

When the tree drops its branches
It is weakened,
When it drops its leaves
It is not weakened:
Leaves will grow again.

When the world loses its resources
It is weakened,
When the world loses its young men
It is not weakened:
Young men will grow again.

1971

α and Ω meet

Death has found the fire
And cooled the light.
When darkness is lighted again
But by imaginings
And the silence is deafening
All the pictures are blurred,
All vision is dying,
When out of the fire comes time's ghost,
He stands, taut in every muscle, and is gone.
Across the pale verandah of night
He goes to snatch the moon,
While black lightning roars silently,
The last ashes in the fire.

Smell the smell of damp grass,
The smell of uncovered earth,
The smell of the skull,
The tremor of touching the dead,
Of lifting a dead arm,
The moment when it drops.

In the labyrinth lurks Dissolution,
A Minotaur awaiting his food.
The great black horror bellows,
Challenging a Theseus who never comes.
He must never get out:
Death, blood, cries the monster,
Red lips brimming over,
Teeth rotten with red flesh,
Face caked with blood,
Death, blood, he cries,
Scaling the great cliff,
Coming nearer.

Life has come to the point of no return;
Do not look back, but only blunder on
Until you meet the monster.

1972

Thought (II)

Thought is the moment
Between the finger and the button,
Between the shot and the impact,
The moment
In which things happen,
Things beyond the orders,
Beyond the General's HQ message,
Beyond the smooth run of routine.

Doubt is the terror of the moment,
A thief on the road along which
Disillusion travels,
The menace of realisation
Of the outcome
Before the deed,
Asking the reason
Why it should be done.

1972

Edifice

Watching and waiting
The old witch looks down,
Death, Life and God
Have tried to convert her
To their causes,
But she is always immovable.
Death said that
He was the lord of all,
For all come to his great kingdom.
But the witch was wise
She defied the god
And turned herself
To immortal stone.
Life tried by saying
He was the wisest of all, for he
Processed all.
But the witch said,
'Death takes and destroys
All Life's work,
And I have proved
Death cannot compare
With my power.'
God was most concerned
With her work.
But she had no heart
And could not be touched.

1971

Dawn breaks over the worn fields

Dawn breaks over the worn fields,
Over the great cross of tangled wire,
The crater and the wheel-less cannon,
Over the broken tanks and rifles.
Again, when Helios has gone
Half his course across the sky
This wreckage will be doubled
And I might die,
Alone in the field
With a bullet through my back,
Not a man lying on his death-bed,
But a corpse in a field,
One more figure on the casualty list
In the general's file.

1972

Statistic

My life is a curtained window,
A refraction of light in the mirror,
I am a flash in a snow-covered field,
Brilliant in brightness,
Not a torch in the mist
But in clear daylight.
I am the herald before the king
In bright silk, overshadowed
And so forgotten.
I am the unidentified face in the album,
A passport name, a reply in a census,
One more figure in the population statistics,
Dead while I am alive,
Only alive when dead
Until the statistics are changed.

1973

Out of the Mist

Half-light on a woman's face
Moving from out of the mist,
Standing in the glare of uncertain hope.
Echoing is the bird and the bomber,
Life and death, mutual
In a strange harmonious rhapsody,
Floating out of the mist.
Into the mist they march
Joyful and inexperienced,
And, when the human bread returns
Upon the cold swift stream of life,
They come, unnatural, broken men
Who never can lift heart or voice again,
Stumbling out of the mist,
Mist that blackens out the false eyes,
Only the true eyes return, glazed,
Devoid of outward sight.
The silent tongues are melted by the mist
But this is superficial: only the eyes matter
And they are gone.
Out of the mist comes my joy and my hope,
Out of the mist comes my curse and my fall.

1973

Index of first lines